POETRY
EXPRESS

James Barry

Nelson Canada

© Nelson Canada,
A Division of Thomson Canada Limited, 1993

Published in 1993 by
Nelson Canada,
A Division of Thomson Canada Limited
1120 Birchmount Road
Scarborough, Ontario M1K 5G4

ISBN 0-17-603938-4

Project Manager: Lana Kong
Developmental Editor: Katrina Preece
Senior Production Editor: Deborah Lonergan
Art Direction: Bruce Bond
Cover Design: Janet Riopelle
Cover Illustration: Paul Rivoche
Series Design: Janet Riopelle

Printed and bound in Canada

67890 / WC / 21098

Canadian Cataloguing in Publication Data
Main entry under title:
Poetry express

(Nelson mini-anthologies)

ISBN 0-17-603938-4

1. Poetry, Modern. I. Barry, James, 1939-
II. Series.

PN6101.P64   1993   808.81   C92-095755-2

Series Review Panel

Table of Contents

1

WHO AM I? Point of View

❷

THE WORLD AROUND

3

THE POEM AS
DRAMATIC MOMENT

THE POEM AS PICTURE:
Shape, Concrete, and
Computer Poetry

5

ANIMAL IMAGERY

6

WORD IMAGES

PREFACE

Poems are tidy word-machines rattling along on wordwheels.

Poems are to be heard. The cadences, emphasis, and tone of the reader's voice give life and meaning to a poem.

Poems are also to be seen. They are images quick-frozen on the page, action translated into words.

Poetry Express presents poems as dramatic moments and as speaking pictures. The writer starts a poem on its journey. Your eyes, voice, and imagination complete the poem. Enjoy these poems as they go humming, strumming, and rattling along.

James Barry

Who Am I?

Point of View

▲▼▶▼▲▼▶▼▼▲▼▶▼▶▲▼▶▼▶▶

A poet makes a comment on life around us
and within us. A poet tells us who we are,
where we have been, and where we might
be going.

▲▼▶▼▲▼▶▼▼▲▼▶▼▶▲▼▶▼▶▶

▲ ▼ ▶ ▼ ▲ ▲ ▼ ▶ ▼ ▲ ▲ ▼ ▶ ▼ ▲ ▲ ▼ ▼ ▶ ▶

I'm Nobody! Who are you?
Are you—Nobody—Too?
Then there's a pair of us!
Don't tell! they'd advertise—you know!

How dreary—to be—Somebody!
How public—like a Frog—
To tell one's name—the livelong June—
To an admiring Bog!

Emily Dickinson

There's poetry all over the place.
Robert Lowell

▲ ▼ ▶ ◄ ▶ ▲ ▼ ▶ ◄ ▶ ▲ ▼ ▶ ◄ ▶ ▲ ▼ ▶ ◄ ▶ ▲ ▶

NOBODY

Nobody loves me,
Nobody cares,
Nobody picks me peaches and pears.
Nobody offers me candy and Cokes,
Nobody listens and laughs at my jokes.
Nobody helps when I get in a fight,
Nobody does all my homework at night.
Nobody misses me,
Nobody cries,
Nobody thinks I'm a wonderful guy.
So if you ask me who's my best friend, in a whiz,
I'll stand up and tell you that *Nobody* is.
But yesterday Night I got quite a scare,
I woke up and Nobody just *wasn't there*.
I called out and reached out for Nobody's hand,
In the darkness where Nobody usually stands.
Then I poked through the house, in each cranny
    and nook,
But I found *somebody* each place that I looked.
I searched till I'm tired, and now with the dawn,
There's no doubt about it—
Nobody's *gone*!

Shel Silverstein

▲ ▼ ▶ ▼ ▶ ▲ ▼ ▶ ▼ ▶ ▲ ▼ ▶ ▼ ▶ ▲ ▼ ▶ ▼ ▶ ▶

LOCKED IN

All my life I lived in a cocoanut.

It was cramped and dark.

Especially in the morning when I had to shave.

But what pained me most was that I had no way

to get into touch with the outside world.

If no one out there happened to find the cocoanut,

if no one cracked it, then I was doomed

to live all my life in the nut, and maybe even die there.

I died in the cocoanut.

A couple of years later they found the

cocoanut,

cracked it, and found me shrunk and crumpled inside.

"What an accident!"

"If only we had found it earlier…"

"Then maybe we could have saved him."

"Maybe there are more of them locked in like

that…"

"Whom we might be able to save,"
they said, and started knocking to pieces every cocoanut
within reach.

No use! Meaningless! A waste of time!
A person who chooses to live in a cocoanut!
Such a nut is one in a million!

But I have a brother-in-law who
lives in an
acorn.

Ingemar Gustafson
Translated from the Swedish
by May Swenson

Poetry is the algebra of the heart.
E.E. CUMMINGS

WHO AM I?

I am neither a communist
nor a nationalist:
I am Vietnamese.
Is it not enough?
For thousands of years
that's what I've been:
Don't you think that's enough?
And Vietnam in flames
and mother who weeps
and youngsters who suffer
and all the terminology we use to kill each other!
O river
we stand on our respective banks
our fallen tears mingling.

Tru Vu
Translated from the Vietnamese by
Nguyen Ngoc Bich, with Burton Raffel and
W. S. Merwin

▲ ▼ ▶ ◀ ▲ ▼ ▶ ◀ ▲ ▼ ▶ ◀ ▲ ▼ ▶ ◀ ▶ ▶

I LEFT MY HEAD

I left my head
somewhere
today.
Put it down for
just
a minute.
Under the
table?
On a chair?
Wish I were
able
to say
where.
Everything I need
is
in it!

Lilian Moore

WHATIF

Last night, while I lay thinking here,
Some Whatifs crawled inside my ear
And pranced and partied all night long
And sang their same old Whatif song:
Whatif I'm dumb in school?
Whatif they've closed the swimming pool?
Whatif I get beat up?
Whatif there's poison in my cup?
Whatif I start to cry?
Whatif I get sick and die?
Whatif I flunk that test?
Whatif green hair grows on my chest?
Whatif nobody likes me?
Whatif a bolt of lightning strikes me?
Whatif I don't grow taller?
Whatif my head starts getting smaller?
Whatif the fish won't bite?
Whatif the wind tears up my kite?
Whatif they start a war?
Whatif my parents get divorced?

Whatif the bus is late?
Whatif my teeth don't grow in straight?
Whatif I tear my pants?
Whatif I never learn to dance?
Everything seems swell, and then
The nighttime Whatifs strike again!

Shel Silverstein

▲ ▼ ▶ ◀ ▶ ▲ ▼ ▶ ◀ ▶ ▲ ▼ ▶ ◀ ▶ ▲ ▼ ▶ ◀ ▶

STARS

in science today we learned
that stars are a mass of gases that burned
out a long time ago only we don't know
that because we still see the glow

and i remembered my big brother donny
said he burned out a long time ago and i asked
him did that make him
a star

Nikki Giovanni

All there is to writing is having ideas.
To learn to write is to learn to have ideas.
ROBERT FROST

FIRST WORDS

when i was small
and gurgled my first words
my sister smiled at me
and told me not to bother trying
'cause nobody listens

Robin Gordon

LITERACY

I'm lernin ta ryte.
I'm learnin ta wryte.
I'm learnen too wright.
I've learned to write.

Matthew Dale

Delight is the chief, if not the only, end of poetry.
JOHN DRYDEN

THE POND

There was this pond in the village
and little boys, he heard till he was sick,
were not allowed too near.
Unfathomable pool, they said,
that swallowed men and animals just so;
and in its depths, old people said,
swam galliwasps and nameless horrors;
bright boys kept away.

Though drawn so hard by prohibitions,
the small boy, fixed in fear, kept off;
till one wet summer, grass growing lush,
paths muddy, slippery, he found himself
there, at the fabled edge.

The brooding pond was dark.
Sudden, escaping cloud, the sun
came bright; and, shimmering in guilt,
he saw his own face peering from the pool.

Mervyn Morris

▲ ▼ ▼ ▼ ▶ ▲ ▼ ▶ ▼ ▶ ▲ ▼ ▶ ▼ ▶ ▲ ▼ ▶ ▼ ▶ ▶

THE WATCHER

on the park bench
(an old man) sits
still
his face shaded by a hat
old worn

watches birds, squirrels
people

brings seeds or nuts
to feed them

his prune face breaks
a smile
for the sparrow peeping thanks

I pass by
and wonder
"who feeds him?"

Becky Gorectke

IT COULDN'T BE DONE

Somebody said that it couldn't be done,
　　But he with a chuckle replied
That "maybe it couldn't," but he would be one
　　Who wouldn't say so till he'd tried.
So he buckled right in with the trace of a grin
　　On his face. If he worried he hid it.
He started to sing as he tackled the thing
　　That couldn't be done, and he did it.

Somebody scoffed: "Oh, you'll never do that;
　　At least no one ever has done it";
But he took off his coat and he took off his hat,
　　And the first thing we knew he'd begun it.
With a lift of his chin and a bit of a grin,
　　Without any doubting or quiddit,
He started to sing as he tackled the thing
　　That couldn't be done, and he did it.

There are thousands to tell you it cannot be done,
　　There are thousands to prophesy failure;
There are thousands to point out to you, one by
one,

The dangers that wait to assail you.
But just buckle in with a bit of a grin,
    Just take off your coat and go to it;
Just start to sing as you tackle the thing
    That "cannot be done," and you'll do it.

Edgar A. Guest

*I'm talking about the smallish, unofficial garden-variety
    poem. How shall I describe it?—a door opens,
        a door shuts.*
                    SYLVIA PLATH

▲▼▶▼▶▲▼▶▼▶▲▼▶▼▶▲▼▶▼▶▲▼▶▼▶▶

DRAWING BY RONNIE C., GRADE ONE

For the sky, blue. But the six-year-
old searching his crayon-box, finds
no blue to match that sky
framed by the window—a see-through shine
over treetops, housetops. The wax colors
hold only dead light, not this water flash
thinning to silver
at morning's far edge.
Gray won't do, either:
gray is for rain that you make with
dark slanting lines down-paper

Try orange!

—Draw a large corner circle for sun, egg-yolk solid,
with yellow strokes, leaping outward
like fire bloom—a brightness shouting
flower-shape wind-shape joy-shape!
The boy sighs, with leg-twisting bliss creating

It is done. The stubby crayons
(all ten of them) are stuffed back
bumpily into their box.

Ruth Lechlitner

▲ ▼ ▶ ▼ ▶ ▲ ▼ ▶ ▼ ▶ ▲ ▼ ▶ ▼ ▶ ▲ ▼ ▶ ▼ ▶ ▶

No longer
    can I give you a handful of berries as a gift,
no longer
    are the roots I dig used as medicine,
no longer
    can I sing a song to please the salmon,
no longer
    does the pipe I smoke make others sit
    with me in friendship,
no longer
    does anyone want to walk with me to the
    blue mountain to pray
no longer
    does the deer trust my footsteps…

Chief Dan George

▲ ▶ ▶ ▼ ▶ ▲ ▼ ▶ ▼ ▶ ▲ ▼ ▶ ▼ ▶ ▲ ▼ ▶ ▼ ▶ ▶

THE KNIGHT

Once upon a time there was a knight who rode
over the hills,
and killed a dragon,
and set fifteen women free
from an enchanter who kept the prisoners in a
    tower
and found a castle where they could live,
and rode on to the desert
where two kings were fighting a war that never
    ended
and waved a magic shield over the battle
so all the soldiers stopped fighting and said,
"What are we here for?"
And then the knight turned and rode back,
through the desert, past the tower, over the hills,
and when she got home
she took off her armour, patted the cat and made
herself a cup of tea

Jenny Pausacker

The World Around

▲ ▼ ▶ ▼ ▲ ▼ ▶ ▼ ▲ ▼ ▶ ▼ ▲ ▼ ▶ ▼ ▶

Poetry is a response to the daily necessity of getting the world right.

Wallace Stevens

▲ ▼ ▶ ▼ ▲ ▼ ▶ ▼ ▲ ▼ ▶ ▼ ▲ ▼ ▶ ▼ ▶

AN ENVIRONMENTALLY SAFE NON-TOXIC POEM

Don't ya just love
how everything is disposable nowadays?
Disposable plastic diapers,
no worry about the mess.
Won't break down for five hundred years.
Styrofoam cups,
just throw them away.
Beats washing dishes.
How bout them holes in the ozone?
Gonna be a disposable planet,
   non-recyclable.

Stephen Johnson

*The only cause for pessimism would be if men and
women ceased to write poetry, and they don't.*
ELIZABETH DREW

▲ ▼ ▶ ▼ ▲ ▼ ▶ ▼ ▶ ▲ ▼ ▶ ▼ ▶ ▲ ▼ ▶ ▼ ▶ ▶

SKIP ROPE RHYME FOR OUR TIME

Junk mail, junk mail,
look look look:
bargain offer coupon,
catalogue book.

Junk mail, junk mail,
free free free:
trial sample,
guarantee.

Here's an offer
you can't let pass:
an artificial lawn
with real crab grass.

Twenty cents off,
just go to the store
and buy what you don't want,
then buy some more.

Junk mail, junk mail,
what's my name?
My name is Dear Occupant
and yours is the same.

Eve Merriam

▲▼▶◀▶▲▼▶◀▶▲▼▶◀▶▲▼▶◀▶▲▼▶▶

CONSTRUCTION

The giant mouth
chews
rocks
spews them
and is back for
more.

The giant arm
swings up
with a girder
for
the fourteenth floor.

Down there,
a tiny man
is
telling them
where
to put a skyscraper.

Lilian Moore

STEAM SHOVEL

The dinosaurs are not all dead.
I saw one raise its iron head
To watch me walking down the road
Beyond our house today.
Its jaws were dripping with a load
Of earth and grass that it had cropped.
It must have heard me where I stopped,
Snorted white steam my way,
And stretched its long neck out to see,
And chewed, and grinned quite amiably.

Charles Malam

A poem
a plea, a pester,
a please,
a package of words

HUNGER

I come among the peoples like a shadow.
I sit down by each man's side.

None sees me, but they look on one another,
And know that I am there.

My silence is like the silence of the tide
That buries the playground of children;

Like the deepening of frost in the slow night,
When birds are dead in the morning.

Armies trample, invade, destroy,
With guns roaring from earth and air.

I am more terrible than armies,
I am more feared than cannon.

Kings and chancellors give commands;
I give no command to any;

But I am listened to more than kings
And more than passionate orators.

I unswear words, and undo deeds.
Naked things know me.

I am the first and last to be felt of the living.
I am Hunger.

Laurence Binyon

▲ ▼ ▶ ▼ ▶ ▲ ▼ ▶ ▼ ▲ ▼ ▶ ▼ ▲ ▼ ▶ ▼ ▲ ▶

A HELPING HAND

We gave a helping hand to grass—
    and it turned into corn.
We gave a helping hand to fire—
    and it turned into a rocket.
Hesitatingly,
cautiously,
we give a helping hand
to people,
to some people ...

Miroslav Holub
Translated from the Czech
by George Theiner

The best words in their best order.
SAMUEL TAYLOR COLERIDGE

▲▼▶▼▶▲▼▶▼▶▲▼▶▼▶▲▼▶▼▶▲▼▶▼▶

DINNER DIARY

October 17:
Travelled fifteen miles.
Made supper
of toasted rawhide
sealskin boots.
Palatable.
Feel encouraged.

October 18:
Travelled all day.
Ate more pieces
of my sealskin boots,
boiled and toasted.
Used sole first.
Set rabbit snares.

October 19:
No rabbit in snare.
Breakfast and dinner
of rawhide boots.
Fine,
But not enough.

October 20:
Breakfast
from top of boots.
Not as good as sole.

Meguido Zola

Inspired by entries in the diary of Bishop
Isaac O. Stringer, written while he was lost in
the wilderness north of Dawson City, Yukon,
in 1909. The diary was found by Meguido
Zola.

MY MOCCASINS

My moccasins have not walked
Among the giant forest trees

My leggings have not been brushed
Against the fern and berry bush

My medicine pouch has not been filled
With roots and herbs and sweetgrass

My hands have not fondled a spotted fawn
My eyes have not beheld
The golden rainbow of the north

My hair has not been adorned
With the eagle feather

Yet
My dreams are dreams of these
My heart is one with them
The scent of them caresses my soul

Duke Redbird

▲ ▼ ▶ ▼ ▶ ▲ ▼ ▶ ▼ ▶ ▲ ▼ ▶ ▼ ▶ ▲ ▼ ▶ ▼ ▶ ▶

WHEN I WAS SMALL

When I was small
I used to help my father
Make axe handles.
Coming home from the wood with a bundle
Of maskwi, snawey, aqamoq,
My father would chip away,
Carving with a crooked knife,
Until a well-made handle appeared,
Ready to be sand-papered
By my brother.

When it was finished
We started another,
Sometimes working through the night
With me holding a lighted shaving
To light their way
When the kerosene lamp ran dry.

Then in the morning
My mother would be happy
That there would be food today
When father sold our work.

Rita Joe

▲ ▼ ▶ ▼ ▶ ▲ ▼ ▶ ▼ ▶ ▲ ▼ ▶ ▼ ▶ ▲ ▼ ▶ ▼ ▶ ▶

TV NEWS

I sat and ate my tea
And watched them die
And knew at twelve
That brave men died
On either side.
And that is why
At twelve I cried—and cried,
And couldn't understand
My father's beaming pride.

John Kitching

▲ ▶ ▶ ▼ ▲ ▼ ▶ ▼ ▶ ▲ ▼ ▶ ▼ ▶ ▲ ▼ ▶ ▼ ▶ ▶

GRANDPA'S STORIES

The pictures on the television
Do not make me dream as well
As the stories without pictures
Grandpa knows how to tell.

Even if he does not know
What makes a Spaceman go,
Grandpa says back in his time
Hamburgers only cost a dime,
Ice cream cones a nickle,
And a penny for a pickle.

Langston Hughes

SWEATERS

Orange, blue, green and grey,
Striped, plaid, patched and zig-zagged,
Scratching, itching, comforting, warming,
Folded away neatly in the bottom drawer.

The dresser was taller than me;
It took me a minute to open the huge drawer.
I'd lift some up,
Move some over,
Take some out,
Smell,
Feel,
And hug them.

Carefully I would fold them
Leaving out the one I had picked
Then I would close the cradle sized drawer,
Skip to where my father sat
In front of the fireplace
And watch him put on the sweater
I had chosen.

Lucy Gray-Donald

▲ ▼ ▶ ▼ ▶ ▲ ▼ ▶ ▼ ▶ ▲ ▼ ▶ ▼ ▶ ▲ ▼ ▶ ▼ ▶ ▶

THE LATE EXPRESS

There's a train that runs through Hawthorn
3 a.m. or thereabout.
You can hear it hooting sadly,
but no passengers get out.

"That's much too early for a train,"
the station-master said,
"but it's driven by Will Watson
and Willie Watson's dead."

Poor Willie was a driver
whose record was just fine,
excepting that poor Willie
never learnt to tell the time.

Fathers came home late for dinner,
schoolboys late for their exams,
millionaires had missed on millions,
people changing to the trams.

Oh such fussing and complaining,
even Railways have their pride—
so they sacked poor Willie Watson
and he pined away and died.

Now his ghost reports for duty,
and unrepentant of his crime,
drives a ghost train through here nightly
and it runs to Willie's time.

Barbara Giles

THE GARDEN YEAR

January brings the snow,
Makes our feet and fingers glow.

February brings the rain,
Thaws the frozen lake again.

March brings breezes, loud and shrill,
To stir the dancing daffodil.

April brings the primrose sweet,
Scatters daisies at our feet.

May brings flocks of pretty lambs
Skipping by their fleecy dams.

June brings tulips, lilies, roses,
Fills the children's hands with posies.

Hot July brings cooling showers,
Apricots and gillyflowers.

August brings the sheaves of corn,
Then the harvest home is borne.

Warm September brings the fruit;
Sportsmen then begin to shoot.

Fresh October brings the pheasant;
Then to gather nuts is pleasant.

Dull November brings the blast;
Then the leaves are whirling fast.

Chill December brings the sleet,
Blazing fire, and Christmas treat.

Sara Coleridge

Art's single greatest potential is—surprise.
GUILLAUME APOLLINAIRE

THE BOX

Once upon a time in the land of hush-a-bye,
Around about the wondrous days of yore,
They came across a sort of box
Bound up with chains and locked with locks
And labeled, "Kindly do not touch, it's war."

A decree was issued 'round about—
All with a flourish and a shout
And a gaily coloured mascot
Tripping lightly on before—
"Don't fiddle with this deadly box
Or break the chains or pick the locks
And please don't ever mess about with war."

Well the children understood,
Children happen to be good
And were just as good around the time of yore,
They didn't try to pick the locks
Or break into the deadly box
And never tried to play about with war.

Mommies didn't either—
Sisters, Aunts, nor Grannies neither
'Cause they were quiet, and sweet and pretty
In those wondrous days of yore,
Well, very much the same as now
And not the ones to blame, somehow,
For opening up that deadly box of war.

But someone did,
Someone battered in the lid
And spilled the insides out across the floor.
A sort of bouncy bumpy ball
Made up of flags and guns and all
The tears and horror and the death
That goes with war.

It bounced right out
And went bashing all about
And bumping into everything in store;
And what was sad and most unfair
Was that it didn't really seem to care
Much whom it bumped, or why,
Or what, or for.

It bumped the children mainly,
And I'll tell you this quite plainly,
It bumps them every day and what is more
It leaves them dead and burned and dying,
Thousands of them sick and crying,
'Cause when it bumps it's very very sore.

There is a way to stop the ball,
It isn't very hard at all,
All it takes is wisdom and
I'm absolutely sure
We could get it back into the box
And bind the chains and lock the locks

But no one seems to want to save the children
    anymore.
Well that's the way it all appears
'Cause it's been bouncing 'round for years and
    years
In spite of all the wisdom wizzed
Since those wondrous days of yore,
And the time they came across that box
Bound up with chains and locked with locks
And labeled, "Kindly do not touch, it's war."

Kendrew Lascelles

3

The Poem as Dramatic Moment

▲▼►▼►▲▼►▼►▲▼►▼►▲▼►▼►▼►▶

A poem is made for the human voice.
These poems are made for dramatic
readings—solo, in duet, or in larger
groups.

▲▼►▼►▲▼►▼►▲▼►▼►▲▼►▼►▶

▲ ▼ ▶ ▼ ▲ ▼ ▶ ▼ ▲ ▼ ▶ ▼ ▲ ▼ ▶ ▼ ▲ ▶ ▶

SIX TONGUE TWISTERS
Anonymous/Gyles Brandreth

1. Peter Piper picked a peck of pickled peppers.
   Did Peter Piper pick a peck of pickled peppers?
   If Peter Piper picked a peck of pickled peppers,
   Where's the peck of pickled peppers Peter Piper
     picked?

2. Betty Botter bought some butter,
   But, she said, this butter's bitter;
   If I put it in my batter,
   It will make my batter bitter,
   But a bit of better butter
   Will make my batter better.
   So she bought a bit of butter
   Better than her bitter butter,
   And she put it in her batter,
   And it made her batter better,
   So 'twas a better Betty Botter
   Bought a bit of better butter.

3. Andrew Airpump asked his Aunt her ailment.
   Did Andrew Airpump ask his Aunt her ailment?
   If Andrew Airpump asked his Aunt her ailment,
   Where was the ailment of Andrew Airpump's
     Aunt?

4. If a woodchuck could chuck wood,
   how much wood would a woodchuck chuck
   if a woodchuck could chuck wood?
   He would chuck, he would,
   as much as he could,
   if a woodchuck could chuck wood.

5. Kimbo Kemble kicked his kinsman's kettle.
   Did Kimbo Kemble kick his kinsman's kettle?
   If Kimbo Kemble kicked his kinsman's kettle,
   Where's the kinsman's kettle Kimbo Kemble
      kicked?

6. The Duke dragged
   the dizzy Dane
   down into the deep
   damp dank dungeon.

TEN SHORT POEMS
Ogden Nash

1. *THE MULES*

   In the world of mules
   There are no rules.

2. *THE BABY*

   A bit of talcum
   Is always walcum.

3. *THE FLY*

   God in His wisdom made the fly
   And then forgot to tell us why.

4. *CELERY*

   Celery, raw,
   Develops the jaw,
   But celery, stewed,
   Is more quietly chewed.

5. *FURTHER REFLECTION ON PARSLEY*

   Parsley
   Is gharsley.

6. *THE TERMITE*

Some primal termite knocked on wood
And tasted it, and found it good,
And that is why your Cousin May
Fell through the parlour floor today.

7. *THE PARSNIP*

The parsnip, children, I repeat,
Is simply an anemic beet.
Some people call the parsnip edible;
Myself, I find this claim incredible.

8. *THE PARENT*

Children aren't happy with nothing to ignore,
  And that's what parents were created for.

9. *THE JELLYFISH*

Who wants my jellyfish?
I'm not sellyfish!

10. *THE KITTEN*

The trouble with a kitten is
THAT
Eventually it becomes a
CAT.

▲ ▼ ▶ ▼ ▶ ▲ ▼ ▶ ▼ ▶ ▲ ▼ ▶ ▼ ▶ ▲ ▼ ▶ ▼ ▶ ▶

Xenobia Phobia
Hates to walk,
Xenobia Phobia
Hates to talk.

Xenobia Phobia
Hates to ride,
She hates the city
And the countryside.

Hates her father,
Hates her mother,
Hates her sister
And baby brother.

Hates her uncles,
All her aunts,
Hates her hamster
And the hanging plants.

She hates the circus,
Hates the zoo,
Hates birthday parties
And the colour blue.

She hates to dance
And hates to sing.
Xenobia loves
To hate everything.

Eve Merriam

▲ ▼ ▶ ◀ ▶ ▲ ▼ ▶ ◀ ▶ ▲ ▼ ▶ ◀ ▶ ▲ ▼ ▶ ◀ ▶ ▶

FOR WANT OF A NAIL

For want of a nail, the shoe was lost,
For want of a shoe, the horse was lost,
For want of a horse, the rider was lost,
For want of a rider, the battle was lost,
For want of a battle, the kingdom was lost.
And all for the want of a horseshoe nail.

Anonymous

▲ ▶ ▼ ▶ ▲ ▶ ▼ ▶ ▲ ▶ ▼ ▶ ▲ ▶ ▼ ▶ ▼ ▶ ▶

THE BEST FIRM

A pretty good firm is "Watch & Waite,"
And another is "Attit, Early & Layte";
And still another is "Doo & Dairit";
But the best is probably "Grinn & Barrett."

Walter G. Doty

▲ ▶ ▼ ▶ ▲ ▶ ▼ ▶ ▲ ▶ ▼ ▶ ▲ ▶ ▼ ▶ ▼ ▶ ▶

TEN PUN POEMS
Ennis Rees

1.   Caesar said he had to admit
   His days in Egypt were a trial.
   But Cleopatra said, "Not a bit."
   You see she lived upon denial.
          (Upon the Nile.)

2.   Said the cop to the crook,
   "This is no way to greet you.
   But here we are—
   Police to meet you!"
          (Pleased to meet you.)

3.　Said he, "I'm the only painless dentist,"
　　And truer words are seldom spoken,
　　For just that morning every window
　　In the office had been broken.
　　　　　　　　(The only paneless dentist.)

4.　The friendly doctor said,
　　"You'd better watch your diet,
　　But what you really need
　　Is a little peach and quiet."
　　　　　　　　(Peace and quiet.)

5.　"Burning love,"
　　Said he, "is cruel.
　　And for it I
　　Have become a fuel!"
　　　　　　　　(A fool.)

6.　"In Mexico,"
　　Said Willy to Wally,
　　"It's chilly today
　　And hot tamale."
　　　　　　　　(Hot tomorrow.)

7. As Mrs. Fairday
   Told her daughter,
   "While playing croquet,
   We must have lawn order."
             (Law and order.)

8. When the amoeba
   Said, "Oh, Willy!"
   The protoplasm
   Said, "Don't bacilli."
             (Don't be silly.)

9. A freighter hailed a steamer
   Just off the Outer Banks.
   When the freighter asked, "Do you need oil?"
   The steamer replied, "No tanks."

10. "Where in the world did you get that coat?"
    "In South Dacoata, from a goat."
    "Well tell me where you got those pants."
    "In Pantsylvania, just by chance."
    "And where, my dear, did you get that vest?"
    "In Vest Virginia. Now don't be a pest."
    "And where did you get that stiff white collar?"
    "In Collarado—one more and I'll holler."
    "Your hat is from Manhattan—yes?"
    "That's right, my dear—how did you guess?"

▲ ▶ ▶ ▼ ▲ ▼ ▶ ▼ ▲ ▶ ▼ ▲ ▶ ▼ ▲ ▶ ▼ ▶ ▶

FIREFLIES

This poem is meant to be read aloud by two readers at once, one taking the left-hand part, the other taking the right-hand part. When both readers have lines at the same horizontal level, they should speak those lines simultaneously.

Light	Light
	is the ink we use
Night	Night
is our parchment	
	We're
	fireflies
fireflies	flickering
flitting	
	flashing
fireflies	
glimmering	fireflies
	gleaming
glowing	
Insect calligraphers	Insect calligraphers
practising penmanship	
	copying sentences

Six-legged scribblers	Six-legged scribblers
of vanishing messages,	
	fleeting graffiti
Fine artists in flight	Fine artists in flight
adding dabs of light	
	bright brush strokes
Signing the June nights	Signing the June
nights	
as if they were paintings	as if they were
paintings	
	We're
flickering	fireflies
fireflies	flickering
fireflies.	fireflies.

Paul Fleischman

▲ ▼ ▶ ▼ ▲ ▼ ▶ ▼ ▼ ▲ ▼ ▶ ▼ ▲ ▼ ▶ ▼ ▶ ▶

HONEYBEES

This poem is meant to be read aloud by two readers at once, one taking the left-hand part, the other taking the right-hand part. When both readers have lines at the same horizontal level, they should speak those lines simultaneously.

Being a bee	Being a bee
	is a joy.
is a pain.	
	I'm a queen
I'm a worker	
I'll gladly explain.	I'll gladly explain.
	Upon rising, I'm fed
	by my royal attendants,
I'm up at dawn, guarding	
the hive's narrow entrance	
	I'm bathed
then I take out	
the hive's morning trash	
	then I'm groomed.
then I put in an hour	
making wax,	
without two minutes' time	
to sit still and relax.	

The rest of my day
is quite simply set

forth:
Then I might collect nectar
from the field
three miles north

I lay eggs,

or perhaps I'm on
larva detail

by the hundred.

feeding the grubs
in their cells,
wishing that *I* were still
helpless and pale.

I'm loved and I'm

lauded,

I'm outranked by none.

Then I pack combs with
pollen—not my idea of fun.

When I've done
enough laying

Then, weary, I strive

I retire

to patch up any cracks
in the hive.

for the rest of the day.

Then I build some new cells,
slaving away at
enlarging this Hell,
dreading the sight
of another sunrise,
wondering why we don't
all unionize.

Truly, a bee's is the	Truly, a bee's is the
worst	best
of all lives.	of all lives.

Paul Fleischman

▲ ▶ ▼ ▶ ▲ ▼ ▶ ▼ ▶ ▲ ▼ ▶ ▼ ▶ ▲ ▼ ▶ ▼ ▶ ▶

TWO VIEWS

Joy to the earth,	Death to the earth,
how lovely and perf.	the sins and the dearth.
Peace to all its lands,	War shapes all its lands,
guided by careful hands.	filled with enemies and clans,
Nature has its wonders,	Haunted by lightning and thunder,
even in the land down under.	how can we survive this plunder?
Flowing like bread and butter	We need help from others
are blessings from nature's mother.	or else we would be smothered.
Happiness she always sends,	If we do not stop to fend,
for we are all happy friends.	the earth would surely end.

Benny Wan

▲ ▼ ▶ ▼ ▶ ▲ ▼ ▶ ▼ ▶ ▲ ▼ ▶ ▼ ▶ ▲ ▼ ▶ ▼ ▶ ▶

In beauty	may I walk
All day long	may I walk
Through the returning seasons	may I walk
Beautifully will I possess again	
Beautifully birds	
Beautifully joyful birds	
On the trail marked with pollen	may I walk
With grasshoppers about my feet	may I walk
With dew about my feet	may I walk
With beauty	may I walk
With beauty before me	may I walk
With beauty behind me	may I walk
With beauty above me	may I walk
With beauty all around me	may I walk
In old age, wandering on a trail of beauty, lively,	may I walk
In old age, wandering on a trail of beauty, living again,	may I walk
It is finished in beauty	
It is finished in beauty	

Anonymous
Translated from the Navajo
by Jerome K. Rothenberg

4

The Poem As Picture

Shape, Concrete, and Computer Poetry

▲ ▽ ▶ ▽ ▲ ▽ ▶ ▽ ▲ ▽ ▶ ▽ ▲ ▽ ▶ ▶

a poet = "a maker"
a poem = "a speaking picture"

Sir Philip Sidney
A Defence of Poetry (1580)

▲ ▽ ▶ ▽ ▲ ▽ ▶ ▽ ▲ ▽ ▶ ▽ ▲ ▽ ▶ ▶

▲ ▼ ▶ ▼ ▶ ▲ ▼ ▶ ▼ ▶ ▲ ▼ ▶ ▼ ▶ ▲ ▼ ▶ ▼ ▶ ▶

Our glass
of grains
runs out
and
T
I
M
E
will tell
if we can
turn it about

Mary Alban Bouchard

▲ ▼ ▶ ▼ ▶ ▲ ▼ ▶ ▼ ▶ ▲ ▼ ▶ ▼ ▶ ▲ ▼ ▶ ▼ ▶ ▶

Eugen Gomringer

▲▼▶◀▼▲▼▶◀▼▲▼▶◀▼▲▼▶◀▼▶▶

SUPERMAN

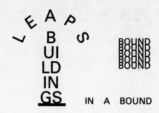

IN A BOUND

Lawrence Yu

▲▼▶◀▼▲▼▶◀▼▲▼▶◀▼▲▼▶◀▼▶▶

NIGHT SONG OF THE FISH

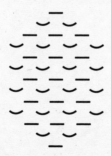

Christian Morgenstern

▲▼▶▼▶▲▼▶▼▶▲▼▶▼▶▲▼▶▼▶▲▼▶▼▶▶

JETSTREAM

A jet screams and climbs

and in a glare
of
blue

a white trail streams across the sky

like the wake
of a
speedboat.

Come!
Ski a sky slope.
Ride a jet tail.

But

HURRY HURRY

Lilian Moore

▲▼▶▼▶▲▼▶▼▶▲▼▶▼▶▲▼▶▼▶▲▶

THE JOURNEY

AIRPLANE   ACCELERATE ——→ TAKE OFF RISING   DISAPPEAR

Gino Yan

▲ ▼ ▶ ▼ ▲ ▶ ▼ ▶ ▼ ▲ ▶ ▼ ▲ ▶ ▼ ▶ ▶

NOVEMBER

```
                                        sun
                                    the
                                    than
Snow                                higher
   and                         fly
      night                 geese
         comes              sky
            down         of
               into    ledge
                  the  yellow
                     last
```

Anne Corkett

*He [the poet] unlocks our chains and admits us to a new
scene.*
RALPH WALDO EMERSON

▲ ▽ ▶ ▶ ▲ ▶ ▶ ▲ ▶ ▽ ▲ ▶ ▽ ▶ ▲ ▶ ▽ ▲ ▶ ▽ ▶ ▶

LIVING AND DEATH

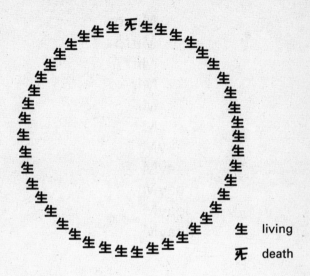

生 living

死 death

Chima Sunada

▲ ▼ ▼ ▶ ▲ ▼ ▶ ▼ ▶ ▲ ▼ ▶ ▼ ▶ ▲ ▼ ▶ ▼ ▶ ▶

REFLECTIONS

Mirror
Mirro
Mirr
Mir
Mi
M
ʏM
ꙅʏM
ǝꙅʏM
lǝꙅʏM
ʇlǝꙅʏM

Colin J. Cunningham

POINT SCORED

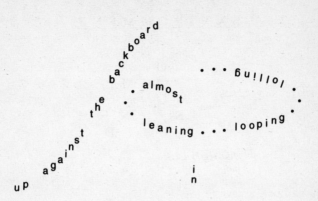

C. Cardenas Dwyer

CLASS

Teacher

!	!	!	!	!	me
?	!	!	!	?	!
?	!	!	!	!	!
!	?	!	–	!	?
!	?	!	!	!	!
!	?	!	?	z	!

John Chun

▲▼▶▼◀▲▼▶◀▼▲▼▶▼◀▲▼▶▼◀▶▶

ENVIRONMENT

E N V I R O N M E N T

<pre>
              N-
           O-
                 M-
           O-
         R-
                    E
</pre>

Joseph Luk

▲▼▶▼◀▲▼▶▼◀▲▼▶▼◀▲▼▶▼◀▶

LATEST ENVIRONMENTAL
PROBLEM

L A T E S T   E N V I R O N M E N T A L   P R O B L E M

<pre>
L   I   P

    S   E   R-

        VI-

    S
</pre>

Steven Lam

▲▼▶▼▶▲▼▶▼▶▼▲▼▶▼▶▼▲▼▶▼▶▶

HISTORY

H I S T O R Y

```
                Y
       IS
       I      T
       HIS
              STORY
```

Peter Park

▲▼▶▼▶▲▼▶▼▶▲▼▶▼▶▼▲▼▶▼▶▶

PHONY

```
F F
A A
C C
E E
D D
```

Domenic Visconti

EMPTY CHAIR

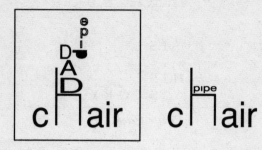

Dennis Yeung

I write half the poem. The reader writes the other half.
PAUL VALÉRY

5

Animal Imagery

A poem is not a destination, it is a point of
departure. The destination is determined
by the reader. The poet's function is but to
point direction. A poem is not the
conflagration complete, it is the first
kindling.

A. M. Klein

▲ ▼ ▶ ▼ ▲ ▼ ▶ ▼ ▶ ▼ ▲ ▼ ▶ ▼ ▲ ▼ ▶ ▼ ▶ ▶

▲ ▶ ▶ ▲ ▶ ▼ ▲ ▼ ▶ ▼ ▲ ▼ ▶ ▼ ▲ ▼ ▶ ▼ ▲ ▼ ▶

THE PURPLE COW

I never saw a Purple Cow,
I never hope to see one;
But I can tell you, anyhow,
I'd rather see than be one.

Gelett Burgess

▲ ▶ ▼ ▼ ▲ ▼ ▶ ▼ ▲ ▼ ▶ ▼ ▲ ▼ ▶ ▼ ▲ ▼ ▶

PURPLE COW

The day I saw a purple cow
While riding on my bike,
I hopped right off and asked that cow
What being one was like.

She gave me such a gloomy look
And cried a purple tear;
Her droopy tail swished slow and sad
Behind her purple rear.

"It's very rude," she softly mooed,
"That no one wants to see you;
And when they do they tell you that
They'd rather see than be you."

"It makes me mad and *mooo*dy,
It makes me sad and bloo;
I *mooo*n around and chew my cud,
That's all I ever doo."

I hopped my bike and rode away
And never went back to see her,
But I can tell you anyhow,
I'd rather see than be her.

Lois Simmie

▲▼▶▼▲▲▼▶▼▲▲▼▶▼▲▲▼▶▼▲▲▶▶

THE WORM

Don't ask me how he managed
to corkscrew his way
through the King Street Pavement
I'll leave that to you.

All I know is
there he was,
circling, uncoiling
his shining three inches,
wiggling all ten toes
as the warm rain fell
in that dark morning street
of early April.

Raymond Souster

▲ ▼ ▶ ▼ ▲ ▼ ▶ ▼ ▲ ▲ ▼ ▶ ▼ ▲ ▼ ▶ ▼ ▲ ▶ ▼

A MOSQUITO IN THE CABIN

Although you bash her,
    swat her, smash her,
and go to bed victorious,
    happy and glorious
    she will come winging,
    zooming and zinging,
    wickedly singing
over your bed.
You slap the air
    but she's in your hair
    cackling with laughter.
You smack your head,
    but she isn't dead—
    she's on the rafter.
She's out for blood—
    yours, my friend,
and she will get it, in the end.
She brings it first to boiling point,
    then lets it steam.
With a fee, fi, fo and contented fum
    she sips it
    while you dream.

Myra Stilborn

ODD

That was
odd
I must
say.

As I sat
on the
stump,
a piece of road
took
a lively
jump.

A small brown
clod
leaped
up
and away.

A piece of road!

Well, it *might*
have been
a tiny
toad.

Lilian Moore

THE FROG

What a wonderful bird the frog are—
When he stand, he sit almost;
When he hop, he fly almost.
He ain't got no sense hardly;
He ain't got no tail hardly either.
When he sit, he sit on what he ain't got almost.

Anonymous

A CENTIPEDE

A centipede was happy quite,
    Until a frog in fun
Said, "Pray, which leg comes after which?"
This raised her mind to such a pitch,
She lay distracted in the ditch
    Considering how to run.

Anonymous

THE PIED PIPER OF HAMELIN
(Excerpt)

Rats!
They fought the dogs and killed the cats,
   And bit the babies in the cradles,
And ate the cheeses out of the vats,
   And licked the soup from the cook's own ladles,
Split open the kegs of salted sprats,
Made nests inside men's Sunday hats,
And even spoiled the women's chats
     By drowning their speaking
     With shrieking and squeaking.
In fifty different sharps and flats.

Robert Browning

THE OLD DOG

What does the old dog say?
Well, here's another day
       To sit in the sun.
And when my master's up,
I'll skip around like a pup,
       And we'll go for a run.
But now, I'll lift my head
Out of my warm bed
       To greet the dawn,
Sigh gently, and slowly turn,
Slowly lie down again,
And softly yawn.

All night I've kept an eye
Open protectingly
       In case of danger.
If anything had gone wrong
I would have raised my strong
       Voice in anger.
But all was safe and still.
The sun's come over the hill,
       No need for warning.
When he comes down the stair
I shall be waiting there
To say Good Morning.

Leslie Norris

▲ ▼ ▶ ▼ ▲ ▼ ▶ ▼ ▲ ▼ ▶ ▼ ▲ ▼ ▶ ▼ ▲ ▶

THE STRAY CAT

It's just an old alley cat
that has followed us all the way home.

It hasn't a star on its forehead,
or a silky satiny coat.

No proud tiger stripes, no dainty tread,
no elegant velvet throat.

It's a splotchy, blotchy
city cat, not a pretty cat,
a rough little tough little bag of old bones.

"Beauty," we shall call you.
"Beauty, come in."

Eve Merriam

▲ ▼ ▶ ▼ ▲ ▼ ▶ ▼ ▲ ▼ ▶ ▼ ▲ ▼ ▶ ▼ ▶

I LIKE CATS

I like cats
because of this known feature...
Each cat is
A complicated creature.

Lola Sneyd

THE PRISONER

I lash and writhe against my prison bars,
    And watch with sullen eyes the gaping crowd…
Give me my freedom and the burning stars,
    The hollow sky, and crags of moonlit cloud!

Once I might range across the trackless plain,
    And roar with joy, until the desert air
And wide horizons echoed it amain:
    I feared no foe, for I was monarch there!

I saw my shadow on the parching sand,
    When the hot sun had kissed the mountain's rim;
And when the moon rose o'er long wastes of land,
    I sought my prey by some still river's brim;

And with me my fierce love, my tawny mate,
    Meet mother of strong cubs, meet lion's bride…
We made our lair in regions desolate,
    The solitude of wildernesses wide.

They slew her … and I watched the life-blood flow
    From her torn flank, and her proud eyes grow dim:
I howled her dirge above her while the low,
    Red moon clomb up the black horizon's rim.

Me, they entrapped … cowards! They did not dare
   To fight, as brave men do, without disguise,
And face my unleashed rage! The hidden snare
   Was their device to win an untamed prize.

I am a captive … not for me the vast,
   White dome of sky above the blinding sand,
The sweeping rapture of the desert blast
   Across long ranges of untrodden land!

Yet still they fetter not my thought … in dreams
   I, desert-born, tread the hot wastes once more,
Quench my deep thirst in cool, untainted streams,
   And shake the darkness with my kingly roar!

Lucy Maud Montgomery

WHY NOBODY PETS THE LION AT THE ZOO

The morning that the world began
The Lion growled a growl at Man.

And I suspect the Lion might
(If he'd been closer) have tried a bite.

I think that's as it ought to be
And not as it was taught to me.

I think the Lion has a right
To growl a growl and bite a bite.

And if the Lion bothered Adam,
He should have growled right back at 'im.

The way to treat a Lion right
Is growl for growl and bite for bite.

True, the Lion is better fit
For biting than for being bit.

But if you look him in the eye
You'll find the Lion's rather shy.

He really wants someone to pet him.
The trouble is: his teeth won't let him.

He has a heart of gold beneath
But the Lion just can't trust his teeth.

John Ciardi

▲ ▶ ▼ ▶ ▲ ▼ ▶ ▼ ▶ ▲ ▼ ▶ ▼ ▶ ▲ ▼ ▶ ▼ ▶ ▶

THE LION IS LOOSE

LION AT LARGE IN SUBURBS
screamed the morning paper
in that bold red lettering
reserved for national emergencies

MANEATER ON THE PROWL
ALL CITIZENS STAY INDOORS
blared the radio announcer
afraid his two police dogs
could not protect him

A LION ESCAPED FROM THE CITY ZOO
TWO DAYS AGO
THE ARMY HAS BEEN CALLED
TO HELP IN THE HUNT
ALL RESIDENTS ARE WARNED
NOT TO APPROACH THE CREATURE
FOR HE IS BELIEVED
STARVED AND DANGEROUS
The six o'clock news signed off
with a picture of the empty cage

As I gazed across my living room at the lion
stretched full on the sofa
I began to think
maybe he had lied to me
and wasn't on vacation after all

David Bittle

THE FIGHT

Jake says: "It's time to teach that colt to drive."
The colt has other plans. *He* says he'll strive

to land old Jake in berry patch or pond.
To tell the truth, he's never been too fond

of even being ridden. It's a drag
you have to put up with. He'd lug or lag

but all it gets you is a whipping. Yet,
he'd love to see old Jake climb, dripping wet,

out of that pond. He'd chance the whip for that!

On Tuesday, Jake, cocksure, hitches up the colt.
No long rein work for him. "He'll never bolt,"

says Jake (whose confidence is seldom low).
"This won't be any kind of fight. He'll go

right where I tell him to. You'll see he will.
I'll take him up beside the pond. Hold still …

Now, off we go… Now, take it easy… WHOA!"

A half mile off they feel the jolt.
Round One: The Colt.

Patricia Hubbell

6

Word Images

▲▼▶▼▶▲▼▶▼▶▲▼▶▼▶▲▼▶▼▲▶

All a poem asks from us is that we come to
it with an open mind. A good poem will
pose its own questions. A poem worth its
hire can sustain a little analysis and
discussion. Press the poem for its insights
and then move on.

▲▼▶▼▶▲▼▶▼▶▼▲▶▼▶▼▲▶▼▶▲▶

▲ ▶ ▼ ▶ ▲ ▼ ▶ ▼ ▲ ▶ ▲ ▼ ▶ ▲ ▼ ▶ ▶

PUZZLED

I took a sip of lemon pop
And then a sip of lime
A little orange soda, too,
A swallow at a time.
Some grape came next and cherry red,
And then I almost cried.
How *could* my stomach feel so bad
With rainbows down inside?

Margaret Hillert

*Poetry is the shape and shade and size of words as they
hum, strum, jig, and gallop along.*
DYLAN THOMAS

▲ ▼ ▶ ▼ ▲ ▼ ▶ ▼ ▲ ▼ ▶ ▼ ▲ ▼ ▶ ▼ ▲ ▶

THE RAINBOW

Even the rainbow has a body
made of the drizzling rain
and is an architecture of glistening atoms
built up, built up.
Yet you can't lay your hand on it
nay, nor even your mind.

D.H. Lawrence

Has any poet or critic successfully defined poetry?
They talk about it in such very different terms
that it is difficult to believe that they are describing
the same activity.
ELIZABETH DREW

WHEN IT IS SNOWING

When it is snowing
the blue jay
is the only piece of
sky
in my
backyard.

Siv Cedering

TIMING

"When do you find the time
to write poems?"
a friend asks.
"Oh!"
I say,
"Whenever the light slips
under
the door, ajar,
at midnight
or the wind
pirouettes in my pine tree
at dawn."

Terry Ann Carter

▲ ▼ ▶ ▼ ▲ ▼ ▶ ▼ ▲ ▼ ▶ ▼ ▲ ▼ ▶ ▼ ▲ ▶

LIKE A TREE

I can not make a perfect world for you;

that would be too artificial.

I am like a leaf on a tree.

I will

have

falls.

But,

like a tree in the Spring

I will always bud with beautiful ideas.

Edna H. King

The ideal reader must be sensitive to words over their whole poetic range, and respond to poetry musically, emotionally, imaginatively.
KATHERINE M. WILSON

▲ ▶ ▸ ▼ ▲ ▼ ▶ ▼ ▲ ▼ ▶ ▼ ▲ ▼ ▶ ▼ ▲ ▶

THE ART OF POETRY

Chained to my desk,
I twiddle my thumbs,
Read an old comic book,
Joker gets away again,
Again.
Stick men
Drawn here and there
Frozen forever,
Like me at my desk.

> I chew on a jube,
> Look at my watch,
> See minutes turn to
> Hours.
> An idea
> Pops
> Into my head
> And I start,

> "Chained to my desk…"

Dominique Brown

▲ ▼ ▶ ▼ ▲ ▼ ▶ ▼ ▲ ▼ ▶ ▼ ▲ ▼ ▶ ▼ ▲ ▶ ▶

THREE HAIKU

CONVERSATION

An umbrella
And a raincoat
Are walking and talking together

Buson

Even before His Majesty,
The scarecrow does not remove
His plaited hat.

Dansui
Translated from the Japanese
by R. H. Blyth

HOKKU

Night is a blue fly,
Its two wings are copper:
Silk dawn, satin dusk.

Everett Hoagland

IF I WERE IN CHARGE OF
THE WORLD

If I were in charge of the world
I'd cancel oatmeal,
Monday mornings,
Allergy shots, and also
Sara Steinberg.

If I were in charge of the world
There'd be brighter night lights,
Healthier hamsters, and
Basketball baskets forty-eight inches lower.

If I were in charge of the world
You wouldn't have lonely,
You wouldn't have clean.
Or "Don't punch your sister."
You wouldn't even have sisters.

If I were in charge of the world
A chocolate sundae with whipped cream and nuts
    would be a vegetable.
All 007 movies would be G.

And a person who sometimes forgot to brush,
And sometimes forgot to flush,
Would still be allowed to be
In charge of the world.

Judith Viorst

*The writer wants his pen to turn stone into sunlight,
language into fire.*
BERNARD MALAMUD

WHAT COLOUR IS LOVE?

What colour is love?

Love is red.
Red like apples in the fall and circus balloons and
sunsets.
Red like new mittens and barns and old brick
houses.
Red like people are.

Love is yellow.
Yellow like the sun in spring and daffodils and
bright new pencils.
Yellow like a golden ring and autumn leaves and
fresh farm butter.
Yellow like people are.

Love is black.
Black like earth in new dug gardens and soft nights
and ravens' wings.
Black like smooth roads and polished shoes and
wood stoves.
Black like people are.

Love is white.
White like snow and clouds and whitecaps on the
     water when it's windy.
White like gulls and Sunday shirts and sheets
     drying outside on the clothesline.
White like people are.

What colour is love?

Dorine Cooper

▲ ▼ ▶ ▼ ▶ ▲ ▼ ▶ ▼ ▶ ▲ ▼ ▶ ▼ ▶ ▲ ▼ ▶ ▼ ▶ ▶

THEY SAY WE DO NOT SHOW
OUR FEELINGS

They say we do not show our feelings.
This is not so.
Everything is within,
where the heart pounds out the richness of our
     emotions.

The face only speaks
the language of the passing years.

Chief Dan George

▲ ▼ ▶ ▼ ▶ ▲ ▼ ▶ ▼ ▶ ▲ ▼ ▶ ▼ ▶ ▲ ▼ ▶ ▼ ▶ ▲ ▶

MODEL T

It coughed
and coughed
while he turned
the starter,
sputtering
until it started.
The driver
leaped into the
smoke-covered monster.
As he drove down
the street,
his car
coughed and
coughed,
causing those in sight
to chuckle
at the ailing
creature.
As the day ended,
the driver
drove the car
to its den
to sleep
until tomorrow.
But for the Model T
there was
no tomorrow.

Richard Delaronde and William Stevenson

▲▼▶▼▶▲▼▶▼▶▲▼▶▼▶▲▼▶▼▶▶

STORM

They're at it again
the wind and the rain
It all started
when the wind
took the window
by the collar
and shook it
with all its might
Then the rain
butted in
What a din
they'll be at it all night
Serves them right
if they go home in the morning
and the sky won't let them in

Roger McGough

*Poetry is the imaginative expression of strong feeling ...
the spontaneous overflow of powerful feelings recollected
in tranquillity.*
WILLIAM WORDSWORTH

▲ ▶ ▼ ▲ ▼ ▶ ▼ ▶ ▲ ▼ ▶ ▼ ▶ ▲ ▼ ▶ ▼ ▶ ▶

REFLECTIONS DENTAL

How pure, how beautiful, how fine
Do teeth on television shine!
No flutist flutes, no dancer twirls,
But comes equipped with matching pearls.
Gleeful announcers all are born
With sets like rows of hybrid corn.
Clowns, critics, clergy, commentators,
Ventriloquists and roller skaters,
M.C.s who beat their palms together,
The girl who diagrams the weather,
The crooner crooning for his supper—
All flash white treasures, lower and upper.
With miles of smiles the airwaves teem,
And each an orthodontist's dream.

'Twould please my eye as gold a miser's—
One charmer with uncapped incisors.

Phyllis McGinley

▲ ▶ ▼ ▶ ▲ ▼ ▶ ▼ ▲ ▼ ▶ ▼ ▲ ▼ ▶ ▼ ▶ ▶

KENSINGTON MARKET

Colours
Colours
Colours everywhere
colours of food
   and
colours of people
music sounding
music pounding
Kensington Market on a Saturday morning.

Every Saturday morning
Mom takes her shopping basket
and we go to Kensington Market
Bananas
yams
pumpkin
mangos
okras
and
"whappen"!
Caribbean scent.

Fish with sad eyes
eels
salmon
snapper
and the pretty parrot
Portuguese/Atlantic
Nuts and dried fruits
Mexican herbs and spices
it's Pacos' store
and "Como estas."
chop suey
fried rice
spices from the east
it's Chinese.

The smell of cloves
drifts down the street
it's coming from
the Indonesian restaurant.

All of these mix with music
the sound of
Soca jamming
and Reggae blasting
"yeah man"!

Colours of food
colours of people
colours of scents
colours of sounds
RED GREEN AND GOLD
Kensington Market on a Saturday morning.

Afua Cooper

▲ ▶ ▶ ◀ ▼ ▲ ▼ ▶ ◀ ▼ ▲ ▼ ▶ ◀ ▼ ▲ ▼ ▶ ◀ ▼ ▶ ▶

THE PAINT BOX

'Cobalt and umber and ultramarine,
Ivory black and emerald green—
What shall I paint to give pleasure to you?'
'Paint for me somebody utterly new.'

'I have painted your tigers in crimson and white.'
'The colours were good and you painted aright.'
'I have painted the cook and a camel in blue
And a panther in purple.' 'You painted them true.

Now mix me a colour that nobody knows,
And paint me a country where nobody goes,
And put in it people a little like you,
Watching a unicorn drinking the dew.'

E. V. Rieu

INDEX OF TOPICS
AND THEMES

The Artist

Childhood

Dreams and Fantasy

Environment

Family

Humour

Identity

Outsiders

War

ACKNOWLEDGEMENTS

Permission to reprint copyright material is gratefully acknowledged. Every reasonable effort to trace the copyright holders of materials appearing in this book has been made. Information that will enable the publisher to rectify any error or omission will be welcomed.

"I'm Nobody! Who are you?" by Emily Dickinson is Poem # 288 from *The Complete Poems of Emily Dickinson*, edited by Thomas H. Johnson, (Little, Brown and Company, 1960). Reprinted under public domain. **Nobody** from *A Light in the Attic* by Shel Silverstein, copyright © 1981 by Evil Eye Music, Inc. Selection reprinted by permission of HarperCollins Publishers. **Locked In** by Ingemar Gustafson translated by May Swenson. © 1967 by May Swenson. Used with the permission of The Literary Estate of May Swenson. **Who Am I?** by Tru Vu from *A Thousand Years of Vietnamese Poetry*, edited by Nguyen Ngoc Bich, translated by Nguyen Ngoc Bich, with Burton Raffel and W. S. Merwin (Knopf). Reprinted by permission of The Asia Society, New York. **I Left My Head** by Lilian Moore reprinted with permission of Atheneum Publishers, an imprint of Macmillan Publishing Company, from *Something New Begins* by Lilian Moore. Copyright © 1975, 1982 by Lilian Moore. **Whatif** from *A Light in the Attic* by Shel Silverstein, Copyright © 1981 by Evil Eye Music, Inc. Selection reprinted by permission of HarperCollins Publishers. **stars** from *Spin A Soft Black Song* by Nikki Giovanni. Copyright © 1971, 1985 by Nikki Giovanni. Reprinted by permission of Farrar, Straus & Giroux, Inc. **First Words** by Robin Gordon first published in *Inkslinger 1985, An Aden Bowman Student Writing Anthology*. Reprinted by permission of Aden Bowman Collegiate, Saskatoon, Saskatchewan. **Literacy** by Matthew Dale first published in *Triple Bronze*. Reprinted by permission of Brebeuf College School, Willowdale, Ontario. **The Pond** by Mervyn Morris from *The Pond*. Published by New Beacon Books copyright © 1973. **The Watcher** by Becky Gorectke first published in *Waking Slow, A Student Writing Anthology*, Vol. 3, 1992, published by Holy Cross High School, Saskatoon, Saskatchewan. Reprinted by permission of the author. **It Couldn't Be Done** by Edgar A. Guest. Reprinted from *Collected Works of Edgar A. Guest*, by Edgar A. Guest, © 1934.

Used with permission of Contemporary Books, Inc. **Drawing by Ronnie C., Grade One** by Ruth Lechlitner first published in 1967 in *Saturday Review*. Permission [to reprint] by Branden Publishing, Boston. **"No longer"** by Chief Dan George from *My Heart Soars* (Hancock House Publishers Ltd., 1974). Reprinted by permission of Hancock House Publishers Ltd. **An Environmentally Safe Non-Toxic Poem** by Stephen Johnson first published in *WindScript 1990* Vol. 8, No. 2, a journal of high school literary and visual art published in Regina, Saskatchewan. **Skip Rope Rhyme for Our Time** from *Fresh Paint* by Eve Merriam (Macmillan Publishing Company). Copyright © 1986 by Eve Merriam. Reprinted by permission of Marian Reiner. **Construction** by Lilian Moore reprinted with permission of Atheneum Publishers, an imprint of Macmillan Publishing Company, from *Something New Begins* by Lilian Moore. Copyright © 1969, 1982 by Lilian Moore. **Steam Shovel** from *Upper Pasture* by Charles Malam. Copyright © 1958 by Charles Malam. Reprinted by permission of Henry Holt and Co., Inc. **A Helping Hand** by Miroslav Holub from p. 21 of *Selected Poems: Miroslav Holub* translated by Ian Milner and George Theiner (Penguin Books, 1967), copyright © Miroslav Holub, 1967; translation copyright © Penguin Books, 1967. Reproduced by permission of Penguin Books Ltd. **Dinner Diary** by Meguido Zola from *Do Whales Jump At Night? and Other Poems*, edited by Florence McNeil (Douglas & McIntyre, 1990). Reprinted by permission of Meguido Zola. **"My moccasins have not walked"** by Duke Redbird from *The Only Good Indian*. Reprinted with the permission of Stoddart Publishing Co. Limited, Don Mills, Ontario. **When I Was Small** © 1978 by Rita Joe from *Poems of Rita Joe* (Abenaki Press, 1978). Reprinted by permission of the author. **TV news** by John Kitching from *A Fifth Poetry Book* (Oxford University Press, 1985). Reprinted by permission of the author. **Grandpa's Stories** by Langston Hughes from *The Langston Hughes Reader* (George Braziller, 1958). Reprinted by permission of Harold Ober Associates Incorporated. Copyright © 1958 by Langston Hughes. Copyright renewed 1986 by George Houston Bass. **Sweaters** by Lucy Gray-Donald first published in *Inscape*, Bishop's College School Literary Magazine 1991-1992 Vol. 10. Reprinted by permission of Bishop's College School, Lennoxville, Quebec. **The Late Express** © 1983 by Barbara Giles from *Upright Downfall: Poems by Barbara Giles, Roy Fuller,* *and Adrian Rumble* (Oxford University Press, 1983). Reprinted by permission of the author. Barbara Giles writes poems both for children and grown ups. She also has written several books for ten year olds. **The Garden Year** by Sara Coleridge is reprinted under public domain. **Six Tongue Twisters:** "Betty Botter" is anonymous, from *The Oxford Treasury of Children's Poems* (Oxford University Press, 1988). "Peter Piper," "Andrew Airpump," "If a woodchuck," "Kimbo Kemble," and "The Duke" used by permission of Sterling Publishing Co., Inc. c/o Canadian Manda Group, P.O. Box 920, Station U, Toronto, Ontario, M8Z 5P9, from *The Biggest Tongue Twister Book in the World* by Gyles Brandreth, © 1978 by Sterling Publishing Co., Inc., Text © 1977 by Gyles Brandreth. **Ten Short Poems:** "Celery" and "The Fly" from *Verses From 1929 On* by Ogden Nash. Copyright 1941, 1942 by Ogden Nash. First appeared in *The Saturday Evening Post.* By permission of Little, Brown and Company. "Mules" from *Verses From 1929 On* by Ogden Nash. Copyright 1950 by Ogden Nash. Copyright © renewed 1977 by Frances Nash, Isabel Nash Eberstadt, and Linell Nash Smith. By permission of Little, Brown and Company. "The Baby" from *Bad Parents' Garden of Verse* by Odgen Nash. Copyright 1931 by Ogden Nash. By permission of Little, Brown and Company. "The Jellyfish," "The Kitten," "The Parent," "Parsley," "The Parsnip," and "The Termite" from *Verses From 1929 On* by Ogden Nash. Copyright 1933, 1935, 1940, 1941, 1942 by Ogden Nash. By permission of Little, Brown and Company. **"Xenobia Phobia"** from *Blackberry Ink* by Eve Merriam (Morrow Junior Books). Copyright © 1985 by Eve Merriam. Reprinted by permission of Marian Reiner. **For Want of a Nail**, anonymous, is reprinted under public domain. **The Best Firm** by Walter G. Doty from *Rainbow in the Sky* by Louis Untermeyer. Reprinted by permission of Professional Publishing Services and the Estate of Louis Untermeyer. **Ten Pun Poems** by Ennis Rees from *Pun Fun* by Ennis Rees (London: Abelard-Schuman). © Copyright 1965 by Ennis Rees. **Fireflies** and **Honeybees** from *Joyful Noise* by Paul Fleischman. Text copyright © 1988 by Paul Fleischman. Selection reprinted by permission of HarperCollins Publishers. **Two Views** by Benny Wan first published in *Triple Bronze.* Reprinted by permission of Brebeuf College School, Willowdale, Ontario. **"In beauty may I walk,"** anonymous—Navajo, is reprinted under public domain. **"Our glass of grains**

runs out" © 1992 by Mary Alban Bouchard. Reprinted by permission of the author. **4 IV** by Eugen Gomringer reprinted by permission of the author. **"Superman"** by Lawrence Yu first published in *Triple Bronze*, Vol. 23, 1992. Reprinted by permission of Brebeuf College School, Willowdale, Ontario. **Night Song of the Fish** by Christian Morgenstern reprinted under public domain. From *A Flock of Words, An Anthology of Poetry for Children & Others* edited by David Mackay (The Bodley Head, 1969). **Jetstream** by Lilian Moore reprinted with permission of Atheneum Publishers, an imprint of Macmillan Publishing Company, from *Something New Begins* by Lilian Moore. Copyright © 1982 by Lilian Moore. **The Journey** by Gino Yan first published in *Triple Bronze*. Reprinted by permission of Brebeuf College School, Willowdale, Ontario. **November** by Anne Corkett reprinted by permission of the author. **Reflections** by Colin J. Cunningham first published in *Triple Bronze*, Vol. 23, 1992. Reprinted by permission of Brebeuf College School, Willowdale, Ontario. **Class** by John Chun first published in *Triple Bronze*, Vol. 22, 1991. Reprinted by permission of Brebeuf College School, Willowdale, Ontario. **Environment** by Joseph Luk first published in *Triple Bronze*. Reprinted by permission of Brebeuf College School, Willowdale, Ontario. **Latest Environmental Problem** by Steven Lam first published in *Triple Bronze*. Reprinted by permission of Brebeuf College School, Willowdale, Ontario. **History** by Peter Park first published in *Triple Bronze*. Reprinted by permission of Brebeuf College School, Willowdale, Ontario. **Phony** by Domenic Visconti first published in *Triple Bronze*. Reprinted by permission of Brebeuf College School, Willowdale, Ontario. **Empty Chair** by Dennis Yeung first published in *Triple Bronze*. Reprinted by permission of Brebeuf College School, Willowdale, Ontario. **The Purple Cow** by Gelett Burgess from *The Burgess Nonsense Book*, copyright 1914. **Purple Cow** from *An Armadillo Is Not a Pillow* © 1986 by Lois Simmie, reprinted with the permission of Douglas & McIntyre. **The Worm** is reprinted from *Collected Poems of Raymond Souster* by permission of Oberon Press. **A mosquito in the cabin** by Myra Stilborn from *A Round Slice of Moon*, Reprinted by permission of the author. **Odd** from *Something New Begins* by Lilian Moore. Copyright © 1975, 1982 by Lilian Moore. Reprinted by permission of Marian Reiner for the author. **The Frog,**

anonymous, is reprinted under public domain. **A Centipede**, anonymous, is reprinted under public domain. **The Pied Piper of Hamelin (Excerpt)** by Robert Browning reprinted under public domain from *The Poetical Works of Robert Browning: complete from 1833-1868 and shorter poems thereafter* (Oxford University Press, 1940). **The Stray Cat** from *Jamboree Rhymes for All Times* by Eve Merriam. Copyright © 1962, 1964, 1966, 1973, 1984 by Eve Merriam. Reprinted by permission of Marian Reiner. **I Like Cats** by Lola Sneyd from the book *Classy Cats* published by Simon & Pierre Publishing Co. Ltd. Copyright © 1991 by Lola Sneyd. Used by permission. **The Old Dog** from *Norris's Ark* (The Tidal Press) by Leslie Norris. Used by permission of the author. **The Prisoner** from *The Poetry of Lucy Maud Montgomery*, edited by John Ferns and Kevin McCabe; Fitzhenry & Whiteside Ltd., Richmond Hill, Ontario. **Why Nobody Pets the Lion at the Zoo** by John Ciardi from *The Reason for the Pelican*. Reprinted by permission of the Ciardi family. **the lion is loose** by David Bittle from *Poets of the Capital* (Borealis Press, 1974). Reprinted by permission of Borealis Press Limited. **The Fight** by Patricia Hubbell reprinted with permission of Atheneum Publishers, an imprint of Macmillan Publishing Company, from *A Grass Green Gallop* by Patricia Hubbell. Copyright © 1990 by Patricia Hubbell. **Puzzled** by Margaret Hillert. Permission granted by Margaret Hillert who controls all rights. **The Rainbow** by D. H. Lawrence from *The Complete Poems of D. H. Lawrence* by D. H. Lawrence. Copyright © 1964, 1971 by Angelo Ravagli and C. M. Weekley, Executors of the Estate of Frieda Lawrence Ravagli. Used by permission of Viking Penguin, a division of Penguin Books USA Inc. **When It Is Snowing** by Siv Cedering. Copyright © 1978, 1993. First appeared in *Colour Poems*. Reprinted by permission of the author. **Timing** by Terry Ann Carter from *Hymn of a Small Machine*, © 1992 by Terry Ann Carter, published by Aarkade Design & Offset Printing, Ottawa, Ontario. Reprinted by permission of the author. **The Art of Poetry** by Dominique Brown first published in *Inscape* Bishop's College School Literary Magazine 1991-1992 Vol. 10. Reprinted by permission of Bishop's College School, Lennoxville, Quebec. **If I Were in Charge of the World** by Judith Viorst reprinted with permission of Atheneum Publishers, an imprint of Macmillan Publishing Company, from *If I Were In Charge of the World and Other Worries* by Judith Viorst.

THE EDITOR

James Barry is Chairman of the English Department at Brebeuf College School, North York, Ontario. He is the editor of the poetry anthologies *Themes on the Journey*, *Departures*, and *Side by Side: Songs and Poems*, as well as an annual student writing anthology, *Triple Bronze*. Besides teaching, his special interests are sports (especially hockey), music, and student writing.